My First Interactive Learning Book

ACTIVE MINDS
Alphabet

· ACTIVE MINDS ·

Alphabet

With Interactive CD-ROM!

Publications International, Ltd.

A a  B b  C c

airplane   **beehive**   **car**

D d  E e

duck   **egg**

F f  G g H h

fish   **galoshes**   **house**

I i J j

ice cream   **jelly beans**

K k  L l  M m

kite   **lollipop**   **mouse**

N n  **O o**  **P p**

night   octopus   parrot

Q q  **R r**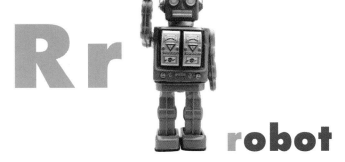

queen   robot

S s  **T t**  **U u**

shoe   truck   umbrella

V v  **W w**

vine   wagon

X x 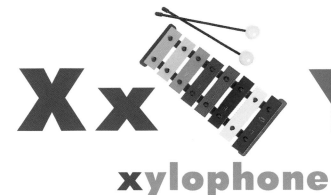 **Y y**  **Z z**

xylophone   yo-yo   zipper

Aa

apple

airplane

bubble

Bb

beehive

clock

Cc

car

duck

drum

Dd

Ee

eraser

egg

flower

Ff

fish

gumball

galoshes

Gg

Hh

house

horse

I i

ice cream

island

jelly beans

J j

jack-in-the-box

Kk

kite

king

Ll lollipop

ladybug

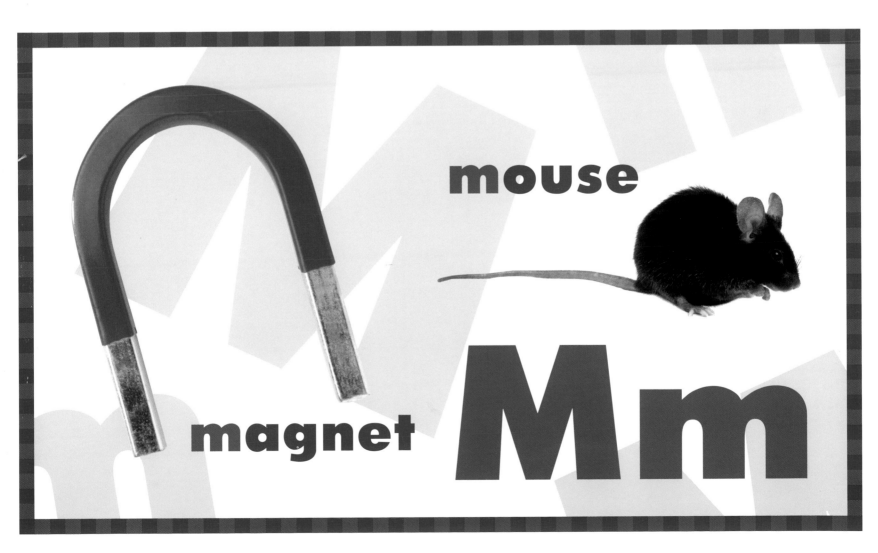

mouse

magnet **Mm**

night

net

Nn

Oo

oil

octopus

Pp

parrot

puzzle

quilt

Qq

queen

Rr

radio

robot

shoe

scissors

Ss

Tt

tree

truck

Uu

umbrella

ukelele

vine

valentine

Vv

Ww

wagon

window

xylophone

Xx

x-ray

Yy

yarn

yo-yo

zipper

Zz

zoo

A a apple

B b bubble

C c clock

D d drum

E e eraser

F f flower

G g gumball

H h horse

I i island

J j jack -in-the- box

K k king

L l ladybug

M m magnet